KV-638-871

Contents

Chapter **1**
The Basics

What is Microsoft PowerPoint?

Microsoft PowerPoint is the leading graphics presentation package. You can use it to create, design and organise professional presentations quickly and easily.

Getting started

▶ Load **Microsoft PowerPoint.** You can do this in one of two ways:

▶ Either double-click the **PowerPoint** icon

▶ Or click **Start** at the bottom left of the screen, then click **Programs,** then click

Microsoft PowerPoint

Your screen will look like the one below:

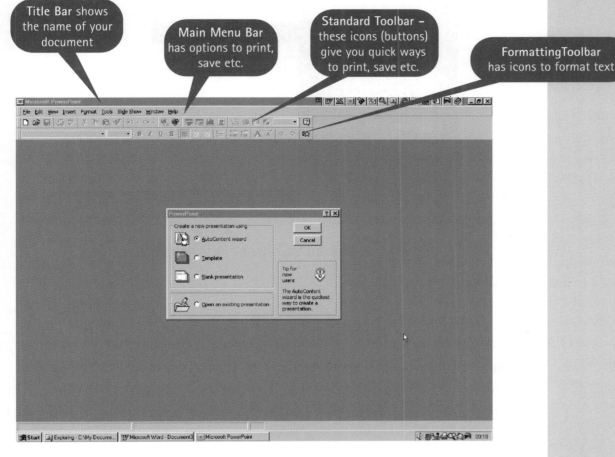

Figure 1.1: The opening screen

The AutoContent Wizard

The **New Presentation** dialogue box appears automatically at the start of a new session in **PowerPoint.** This is the smaller window in the picture above.

The **AutoContent Wizard** is the quickest way to produce a simple presentation because it does all the planning for you.

In this chapter you will use it to produce a simple presentation advertising a school sports day.

 Make sure the **AutoContent Wizard** is selected.

 Click **OK.**

You will see the dialogue box shown in Figure 1.2 below:

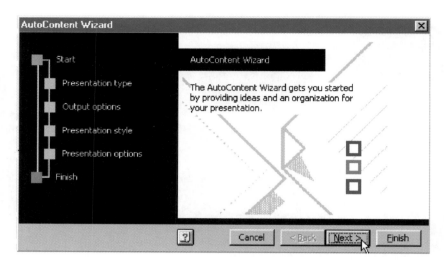

Figure 1.2: The AutoContent Wizard dialogue box

The flowchart on the left of the screen shows you that you are at the **Start**, and in the next few dialogue boxes you will be asked to choose a **Presentation type, Output options** and so on. Keep your eye on the green box in the flowchart, which tells you where you are.

Click **Next** to go to the next dialogue box, where you will choose a **Presentation type.**

Select **General** from the list of buttons.

Click **Generic** in the right hand list box and then click **Next.**

Tip:

If you make a mistake you can always go back a step by clicking the **Back** button.

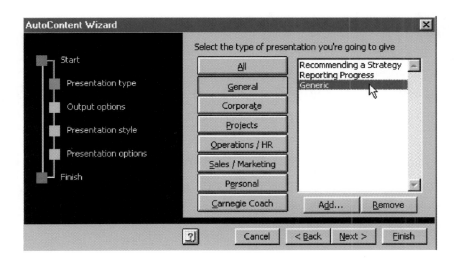

Figure 1.3: Selecting a Presentation type

The **Output options** dialogue box asks **How will this presentation be used?** Select **Presentations, Informal meetings, handouts.** Click **Next.**

In the **Presentation style** dialogue box select **On–Screen presentation.** Select **No** for handouts. Click **Next.**

In the **Presentation options** dialogue box you will enter information for your title slide. See the figure below for an example. You can add your school name as part of the additional information.

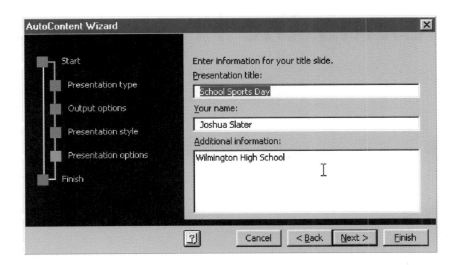

Figure 1.4: Presentation Options – Entering event details

Tip:
In a later presentation you may want to provide **handouts** for your audience to take home and help them remember everything. Handouts also help the audience to follow what you are saying and take notes on specific slides.

Once you have entered your details, click **Next**. Click **Finish** to build your presentation.

You will then see your presentation in **Outline View.** (The **Status bar** at the bottom of the screen tells you this!)

Your title screen appears in a **Presentation window** in the right hand corner of your screen. This is how it will look when it is run. The text on the left of the screen is the skeleton of your presentation.

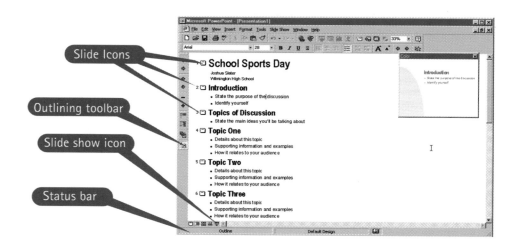

Figure 1.5: The Presentation in Outline view

Viewing the Presentation

Want to see the show so far?

 Click the **Slide Show** icon (see figure 1.5)

 Click the mouse to go to the next slide. You'll see that this slide and all the others need to be edited by you.

Press **Escape** to stop viewing the slides and return to Outline view.

Adding your own content

The suggested topics for each slide might be useful for a future presentation, but they are not much help here. You need to have a plan in your head or on paper of what you are going to put on each slide. This time, that's been done for you!

▶ Replace the heading text **'Introduction'** on Slide 2 by dragging the mouse pointer over the word (or double-clicking it) to highlight it and over-typing with the following: **'10th Annual Junior Games'.**

▶ Replace the next two lines with the time and date: **'12:00pm – 4:00pm on the 25th of June'**, and the location: **'The Main Field'.**

▶ On Slide 3, replace the heading text with **'Events'.** Replace the text on the following line with **'100, 200 & 400 Metres'** and then press **Enter.**

Pressing **Enter** will give you another blank line in which to type in another event.

▶ Enter two more events of your choice.

Deleting unwanted slides

▶ Select Slides 4-9 ready to be deleted. To do this hold your mouse pointer just before the **T** of **Topic 3** on Slide 4 and drag down across the text to the bottom.

▶ You can then delete the unwanted slides by selecting **Edit, Delete Slide,** or by pressing the **Delete Key.**

▶ Now you have finished your presentation. Click the **Slide Show** icon to view it. Click the mouse to change slides.

Your presentation should look like the one in Figure 1.6.

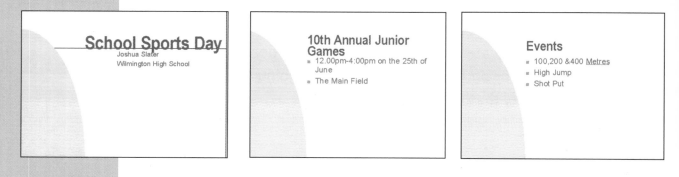

Figure 1.6: The finished slides

Saving your presentation

▶ Click **File** on the menu bar and select **Save.** Save it as **Sports.ppt** – you don't need to type the file extension **.ppt,** which **PowerPoint** will add automatically.

▶ You can now close the file without losing your work by selecting **File, Close** from the menu.

Chapter 2
Template Wizard

Over the next several chapters you'll be working on a longer presentation. It is the sort of topic that you might be asked to prepare and deliver in one of your classes at school. Having **PowerPoint** to help you will make it a whole lot easier to prepare and deliver!

Project: Prepare a slide presentation to be delivered on a computer screen on the topic of 'Building styles in the village of Coddenham'.

Planning a presentation

To deliver an effective presentation you need to consider who your audience is, and prepare your slides to suit them. The audience could be your classmates, your teachers or even the general public at an Open Day.

Whoever your presentation is for, here are a few basic guidelines:

▶ Start with a title screen showing what the project is about.

▶ Don't put more than 4 or 5 points on each slide. People can't concentrate on too much information at once.

▶ Keep each point short and simple. You may want to talk around each point to explain it in further detail.

▶ Sound, graphics and animation can add interest, but don't overdo them!

The Template Wizard

You have already seen the **AutoContent wizard.** Another way to create a quick and colourful presentation is to use the **Template Wizard.**

 Load **Microsoft PowerPoint.** You will see the following screen:

Note:
If **PowerPoint** is already running, select **File, New,** from the menu and click on the **Presentation Designs** Tab.

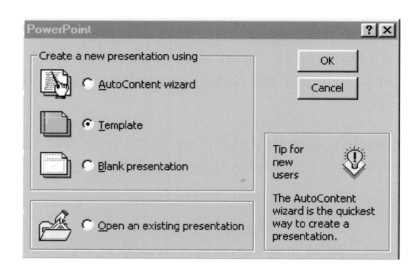

Figure 2.1: Selecting the Template Wizard

 Select **Template** and click **OK.**

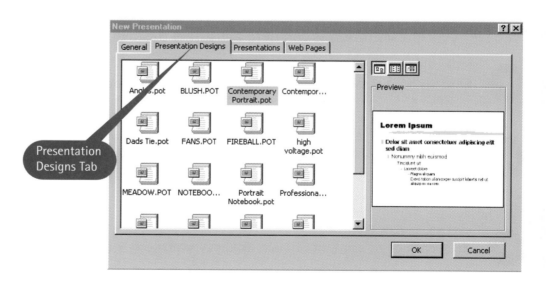

Figure 2.2: The Presentation Designs tab and selected design

Select the **Contemporary Portrait** template and click **OK.**

 In the **New Slide** dialogue box, choose the first **AutoLayout** from the selection. This is the most suitable layout for the title page of your new presentation.

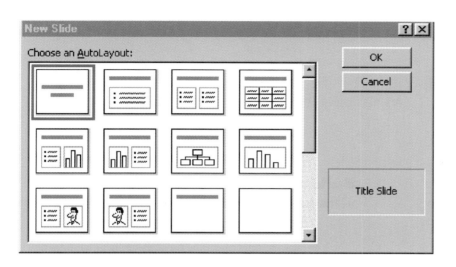

Figure 2.3: Various layout options

 Click **OK.**

Save your new blank presentation as **Buildings.ppt**

Placeholders

Each slide layout displays **placeholders** that allow you to easily add objects such as text, a clip art image or a chart to a slide.

Tip:
It is always important to save your work at regular intervals to make sure that you don't lose too much if something unexpected happens, such as a power cut.

Adding text to the title screen

▶ Click the Title placeholder (where **PowerPoint** tells you to click) and type the title **'Building styles in the village of Coddenham'.**

▶ Now type a sub-title. Click where indicated, and type: **'An historical look at building styles through the ages'.**

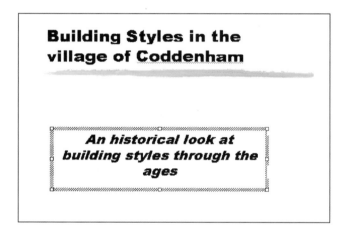

Figure 2.4: Adding text to your title screen

Formatting and moving the text

You can click the text boxes to move them around the screen. You can also format the text in each text box – for example, change its colour, size or alignment.

To format text you need to select the text box by clicking its border. When the border has changed from a diagonal striped box to a fuzzy one you know you can start formatting the text.

If you want to edit, add or delete text in a box, click inside the box. The border changes to diagonal stripes.

Figure 2.5: Formatting box pattern

▶ Select the sub-title text box.

▶ Centre the sub-title by clicking on the **Centre** button. —————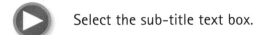

▶ Now make the text Italic by clicking on the **Italic** button. —————

▶ Click and drag the border of the text box to move it into the centre of the slide.

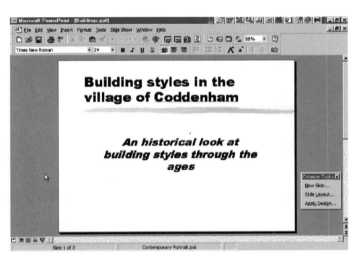

Figure 2.6: The title screen in Slide view

Changing the view

You can alternate between various views of the presentation by clicking on the icons at the bottom of the screen.

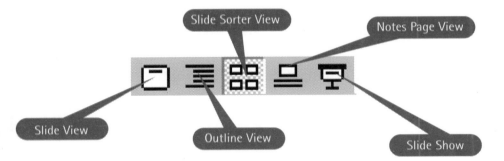

Slide View

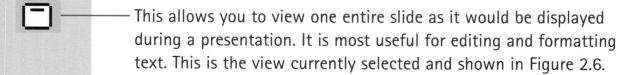

This allows you to view one entire slide as it would be displayed during a presentation. It is most useful for editing and formatting text. This is the view currently selected and shown in Figure 2.6.

Outline View

This is useful for looking at the structure of your presentation. You can also edit text in this mode and view all your screens in the smaller window by clicking on the slide headings.

Click the **Outline View** button at the bottom of the screen.

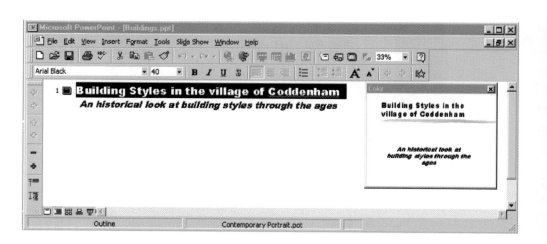

Figure 2.7: Outline view

Slide Sorter View

This view helps you to organise your slides in later stages. We'll be looking at this view later when you have more than one slide.

Here's a preview of what it will look like when you have 6 slides:

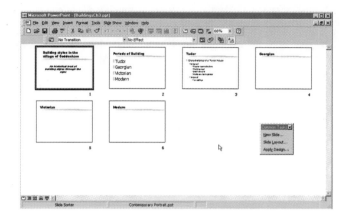

Figure 2.8: Slide Sorter view

Notes Page View

You will be using this in Chapter 7. ————————————

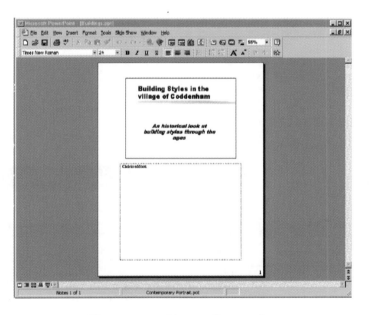

Figure 2.9: Notes Page view

Tip:
You will be returned to the previously selected view after the last slide has been shown.
You can press **Escape** (the key marked **Esc**) at any time during a presentation to end it.

Slide Show

 Click this icon to view your presentation. ————————

 Save and close the presentation.

Chapter 3
Editing a Show

In this chapter you'll add some more to the presentation you started in Chapter 2. You will also be able to change the order of your bullet points and swap the slides around.

Opening an existing presentation

▶ Load **PowerPoint.**

▶ Select **Open an existing presentation. Click OK.**

▶ Note: If **PowerPoint** is already running, click **File, Open...** on the main menu.

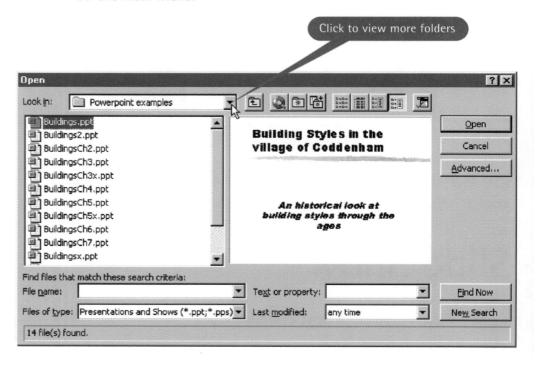

Figure 3.1: Opening an existing presentation

If you cannot see your filename, you can click the small downward arrow in the **Look In:** box. This will bring up a list of folders for you to search.

▶ Click the **Buildings.ppt** file that you created earlier and click Open.

▶ Change to Outline view by pressing the **Outline View** button at the bottom of the screen.

Starting a new slide

Now you can begin the second slide of the presentation.

▶ Click the **New Slide** icon on the Standard toolbar.

▶ The second layout, **Bulleted List** is already selected for you by **PowerPoint.** Click **OK.**

▶ Click the **Slide View** button at the bottom of the screen to go to Slide view.

▶ Enter the text as on the following screenshot, remembering to press **Enter** each time you need to start a new point.

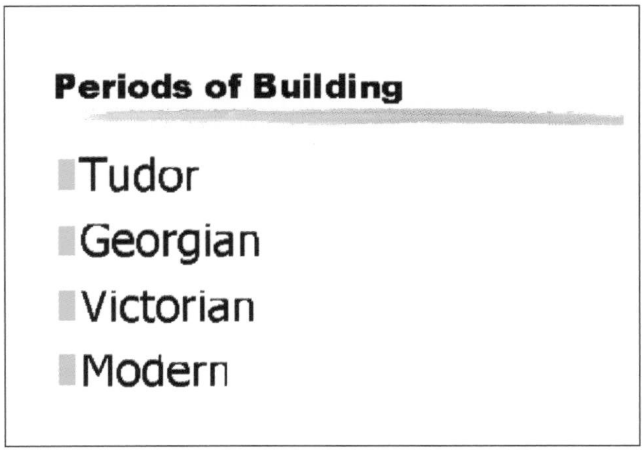

Periods of Building

■Tudor
■Georgian
■Victorian
■Modern

Figure 3.2: Slide 2

Changing text size

You can increase or decrease the size of the text by using the **Font Size** button on the Formatting toolbar. **PowerPoint** also has special buttons for shrinking or enlarging the font one size at a time.

 Select all of the bulleted text on the current slide.

 Click several times on the **Increase Font Size** button to increase the size of the text. The button is located towards the right hand end of the Formatting toolbar.

Your screen should now look something like the one below.
(The text in this screen has been enlarged four or five times.)

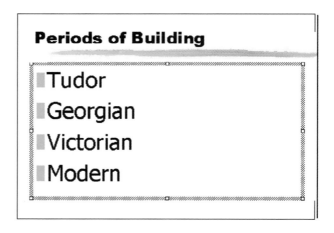

Periods of Building

■Tudor
■Georgian
■Victorian
■Modern

Figure 3.3: Increasing the size of the text

Checking your spelling

You can check your spelling either by using the main menu commands or by clicking the **Spelling and Grammar** button, which you will now do.

▶ Click the **Outline View** button. ─────────────────

▶ Click the **Spelling and Grammar** button on the left of the ───── Standard toolbar.

▶ **PowerPoint** will try to correct all the words it has underlined in red. It should find **Coddenham.** Don't change this to **codename!**

▶ Close the dialogue box.

Expanding a slide

The next four slides are going to show more detail about each of these styles of building. To save typing out these points again as headings on following slides you can tell **PowerPoint** to do it for you and create all the new slides at the same time.

 Make sure you are in Outline view.

 Select Slide 2 by clicking its icon.

 Select **Tools, Expand Slide** from the menu. This will create your new slides. If you had no problems, skip ahead to check that your screen looks like Figure 3.5.

Note:

This may not be possible in some versions of PowerPoint! If you have difficulty, see instructions after Figure 3.4.

Emma, Fee and Robin are having fun with the spell checker. They have typed in their school friend's name **Gary Payne.**

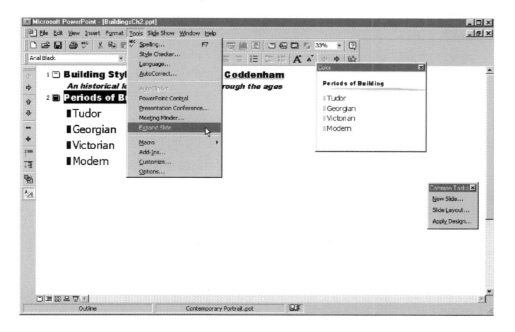

Figure 3.4: Expanding Slide 2

If you had trouble expanding the slides, do this instead:

▶ Click the **New Slide** icon on the Standard toolbar.

▶ Select the **Bulleted List** layout as before and click **OK.**

▶ Type **Tudor.** Press **Enter.**

▶ Add 3 more new slides with titles **Georgian,**
   Victorian, Modern.

You should now have four new slides, each with their own headings.

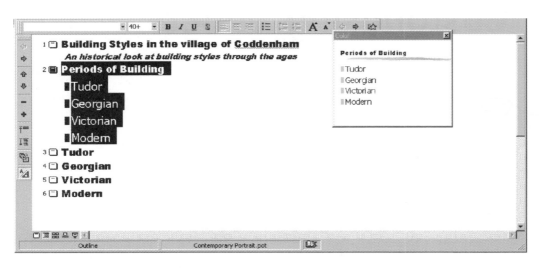

Figure 3.5

Tip:
If you are ever unsure about what a button does, hold your mouse pointer over it for a second and a **Tool Tip** will appear telling you what the button is called.

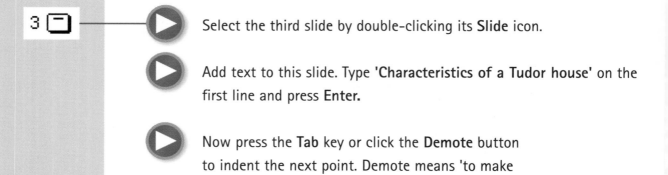

Select the third slide by double-clicking its **Slide** icon.

Add text to this slide. Type **'Characteristics of a Tudor house'** on the first line and press **Enter.**

Now press the **Tab** key or click the **Demote** button to indent the next point. Demote means 'to make less important'.

The Promote and Demote buttons

Your screen should now look like this:

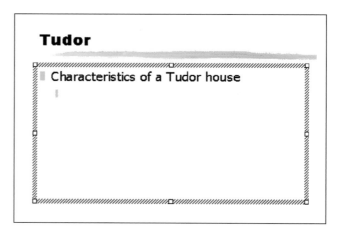

Tudor

Characteristics of a Tudor house

Figure 3.6: Demoting new bullet points

Customising bullets

You can change the style and colour of bullets to increase the impact of a subset of points.

Click **Format, Bullet...** on the menu and select orange as the new colour. Select a new shape for your bullet. Click **OK.**

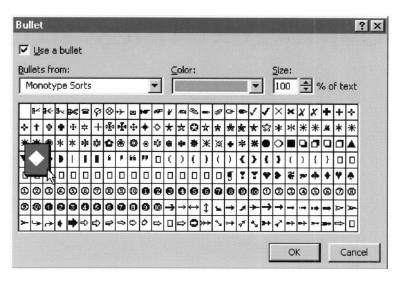

Figure 3.7: Changing the appearance of bullets

▶ The bullet will change to orange as soon as you type some text. Type **External** and then press **Enter.**

▶ Press the **Tab** key or click the **Demote** button to indent the next point.

▶ Type the three external features as shown in the screenshot below.

▶ Click the **Promote** button before typing **Internal.**

▶ Click the **Demote** button and then type the rest of the text as shown below.

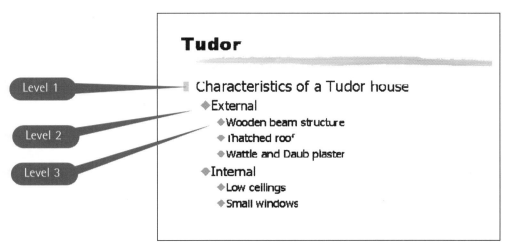

Figure 3.8: Demoting points – Levels 1, 2 and 3

Moving text lines around

The Tudor feature, **'Small windows'** should really be under **External.** Move it up to its proper place as follows:

Press the **Outline View** button to return to Outline view.

Click the mouse pointer to the left of **'Small windows'** and you will see a four-headed arrow style pointer. Hold the mouse down and begin to drag upwards. A line will appear across the screen. Keep going up until the line is underneath **'Thatched Roof'** and let go.

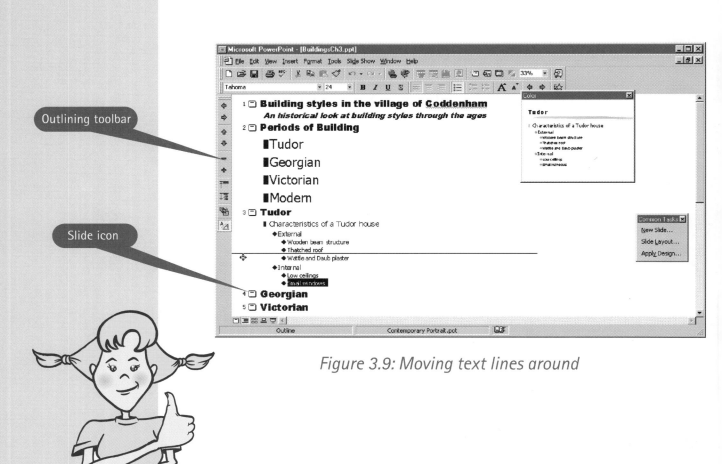

Figure 3.9: Moving text lines around

Tip:
An alternative way to move text up or down the view is to select the line and then click the **Move Up** and **Move Down** buttons on the Outlining toolbar shown in figure 3.9.

The text should have moved up the slide. You can move text from one slide to another in the same way.

▶ Click to the left of **Characteristics of a Tudor house.** Everything in this paragraph will automatically be selected.

▶ Drag downwards to put the text into the slide for **Georgian.**

▶ You don't really want it there, so click **Undo.** The **Undo** button is on the Standard toolbar at the top of your screen.

Changing the order of slides

▶ Try moving the Slide 4, **Georgian** to below Slide 5, **Modern.**

▶ Click **Undo.**

Hint:
Click and drag
the **Slide 4** icon.

Checking your presentation

You can view your progress so far. Look at it first in Slide Sorter view.

▶ Click the **Slide Sorter View** button at the bottom of the screen. —

When you click the **Slide Show** button, the presentation starts at the selected slide (the one with a black border).

 Click the first slide to select it.

Click the **Slide Show** button at the bottom of the screen.

Click or press the **Space bar** to move to the next slide. (Pressing the **Backspace** key goes back one slide. Remember you can cancel your presentation at any time by pressing the **Esc** key.)

Take a break!

Save your work using the **Save** icon.

Close the presentation.

Chapter **4**
Applying Designs

Now you're ready to think more about the overall appearance of your slides. Some slides may need a brighter background than others to increase their impact, or you may want to change the design template. Whatever your ideas, **PowerPoint** has many functions for customising the way you want your slides to look.

Changing the Design Template

▶ Select **File, Open** to open the file named **Buildings.ppt.**

▶ Select **Format, Apply Design...** from the menu.

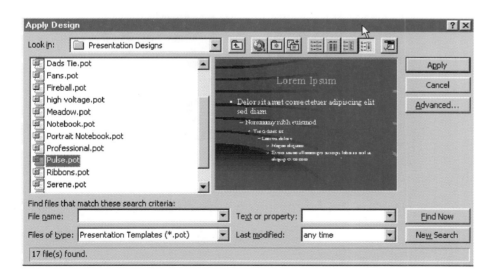

Figure 4.1: Selecting a new Design Template

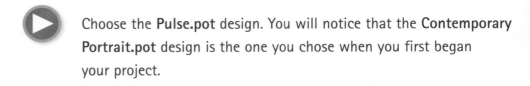 Choose the **Pulse.pot** design. You will notice that the **Contemporary Portrait.pot** design is the one you chose when you first began your project.

Click **Apply.**

Make sure you are in Outline view, by clicking the **Outline View** button if necessary.

Now **double-click** the icon for the Title slide, **Slide 1.** You will notice that the text is still there but you have given the slides a different look. (You may need to reposition the sub-title.)

Note:
In some **PowerPoint** designs, the Title slide has a graphic which is not displayed on the other slides.

Changing the Slide Colour Scheme

With any slide selected, choose **Format, Slide Colour Scheme...** from the menu.

Tip:
This changes the colour scheme in all the slides. To change just the selected slide, click **Apply** instead of **Apply to All.**

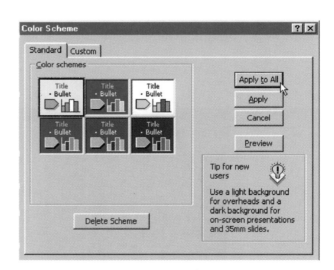

Figure 4.2: Changing the slide colour scheme

Select the top-left design and click the **Apply to All** button.

You can also try customising your own slide using the **Custom** tab.

Changing the background styles and colours

It is possible to change the styles and colours of the backgrounds in your slides without making any changes to the text colours or designs.

 In Outline view, select Slide 1 by clicking on the Slide icon next to it.

Choose **Format, Background** from the menu bar.

Now click the small **down-arrow** beside the 'colour' box.

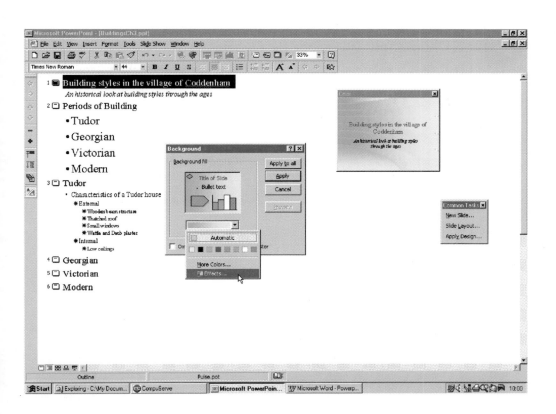

Figure 4.3: Changing the slide background

Click **Fill Effects...** from the drop-down menu.

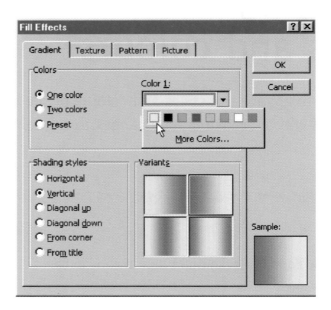

Figure 4.4: Applying a One color gradient effect to a slide background

 With the **Gradient** tab selected, click **One Color.**

 Change **Color 1** to the palest blue and click **OK.**

 Click **Apply.** This will change the background on just the Title slide because it was pre-selected earlier. Click the **Slide View** button to see your changes.

Tip:
You can scroll through all your slides using the scroll bar.

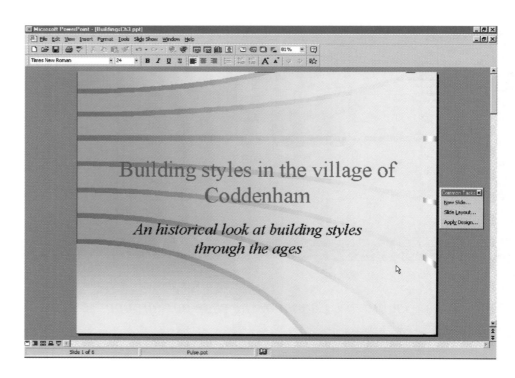

Figure 4.5: The new Title screen background

You can also add textures or patterns to your slides in the same way by clicking on the **Texture** or **Pattern** tabs (See Figure 4.4).

If you have a picture of your own that you would like to see as a background for your slide, you can add it by selecting the **Picture** tab. (This is an advanced feature which will not be covered in this book.)

Changing the layout of a slide

PowerPoint allows you to choose between a number of layouts for each slide. Some layouts are suitable for slides with bullet points, others for slides which will include clip art or photographs, and others for slides showing charts or graphs.

 In Outline view, select the fourth slide titled **Georgian.**

 To select a new layout choose **Format, Slide Layout...**

 Select the layout named **2 Column Text** as shown below. Click **Apply.**

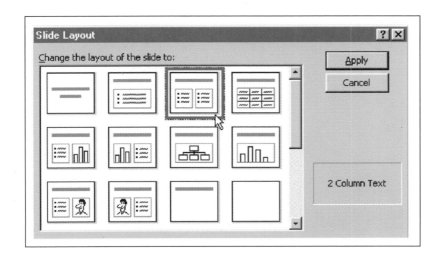

Figure 4.6: Selecting a new layout

Tip:
It is important to select the correct layout for a slide before you add any objects. An **object** is usually a picture or chart.

Your screen should now look like the one below.

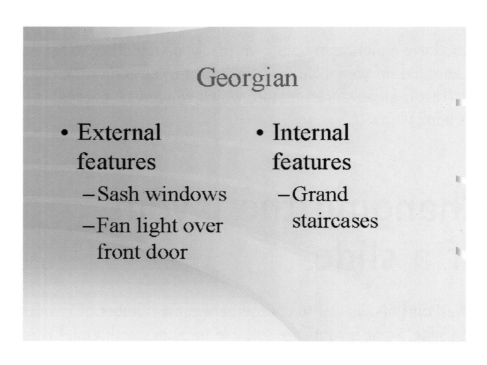

Figure 4.7: Column Text

Make the text bigger by selecting it and clicking the **Increase Font Size** button.

Choosing a layout to include Clip Art

The fifth slide will have a picture as well as text, so first you must change its layout.

 In Outline view, select the fifth slide titled **Victorian.**

 Click **Format, Slide Layout...**

 Select the layout named **Text & Clip Art** as shown below. Click **Reapply.**

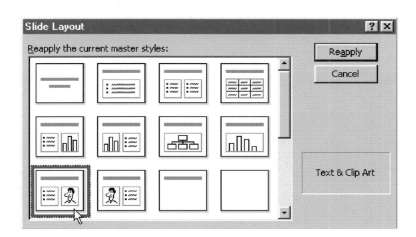

Figure 4.8: Text & Clip Art Layout

You will learn how to use Clip Art in the next chapter.

 Save and close your presentation.

Chapter 5
Adding Objects

You can add pictures, scanned photographs or cartoons to your documents. You can even put in graphs and charts.

▶ If it is not already on screen, open the presentation called **Buildings.ppt**.

▶ In Outline view, double-click the fifth Slide icon or press the **Slide View** button and scroll down to view the **Victorian** slide.

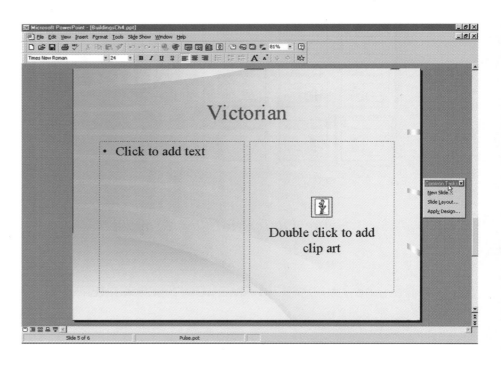

Figure 5.1: Slide 5 in Slide view

▶ Click where indicated to add text and type **'External Features'**.
Press **Enter.**

▶ Press the **Tab** key or click the **Demote** button. Add the sub-points:
Sash windows, Decorated bargeboard and **White brick
construction.**

Changing spacing

Instead of increasing text size to fill the slide, you can increase the
spacing between the three points.

▶ Highlight the text and click the **Increase Paragraph Spacing** button
on the Formatting toolbar.

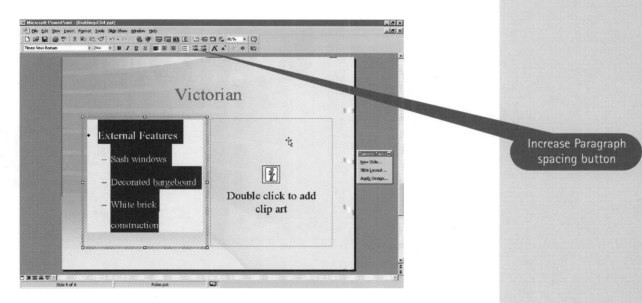

Figure 5.2: Increasing paragraph spacing

▶ With the text still selected, press the **Increase Font Size** button.

▶ Adjust the spacing again if necessary.

Inserting a Clip Art image

You may have a CD with some clip art you can use. Clip art is simply a collection of pictures and drawings that have been drawn by professional artists and collected together for other people to use. **PowerPoint** comes with a small collection of clip art.

▶ Double-click where shown (on the **placeholder**) to add a clip art image.

▶ You will probably see a message telling you that there are more pictures available on a CD. Just click **OK.**

▶ From the **Clip Art** tab, select the **Buildings** category and choose the **door** picture.

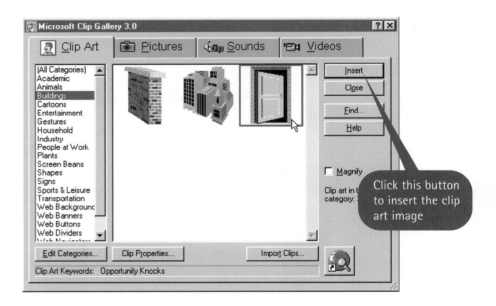

Figure 5.3: Choosing a Clip Art image

Note:

The range of clip art available with the **PowerPoint** package is fairly narrow. In this example a door has been used to help you imagine a house, but you may find something better. You may also have a slightly different selection of pictures to choose from.

Click the **Insert** button to the right of the pictures (not **Insert** on the main menu).

The picture of the door will appear on your slide.

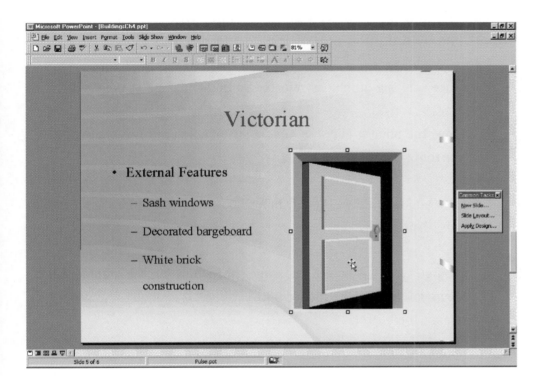

Figure 5.4

 Note the little squares surrounding the graphic (picture). These are called handles. When the handles are visible, the graphic is **selected.**

 Click away from the graphic and the handles disappear.

 Click anywhere inside the graphic and the handles will be visible again.

Changing the size of the graphic

You can make the graphic bigger or smaller without changing its proportions by dragging any of the corner handles.

 Make sure the graphic is selected so that the handles are visible.

▶ Move the pointer over the middle left handle until it is shaped like a horizontal two-headed arrow.

▶ Click and hold down the left mouse button. The pointer changes to a cross-hair.

▶ Drag outwards. A dotted rectangle shows how big the graphic will be when you release the mouse button. When it is about 1cm wider, release the button.

▶ **Save** your work so far.

Adding a chart

Slide 6 would be created in a similar way. You can complete Slide 6 on your own if you have time, putting in some features of a modern house and maybe some suitable clip art.

Next, add a new slide to put a graph on.

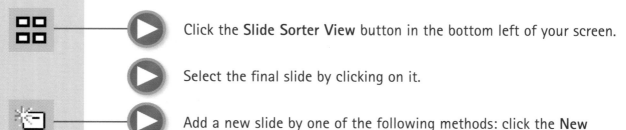

▶ Click the **Slide Sorter View** button in the bottom left of your screen.

▶ Select the final slide by clicking on it.

▶ Add a new slide by one of the following methods: click the **New Slide** icon, or use the menu option **Insert, New Slide...** or click **New Slide** on the Common Tasks toolbar (see figure 5.5).

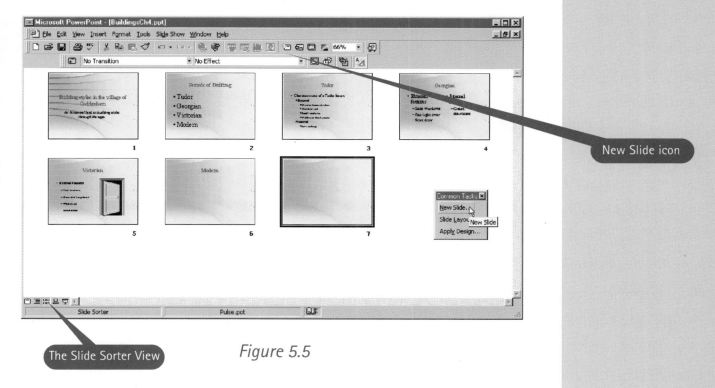

The Slide Sorter View

Figure 5.5

On this new slide you are going to create a chart to show the number of Tudor, Georgian and Victorian houses in Coddenham.

Select the **Chart** layout from the slide choices.

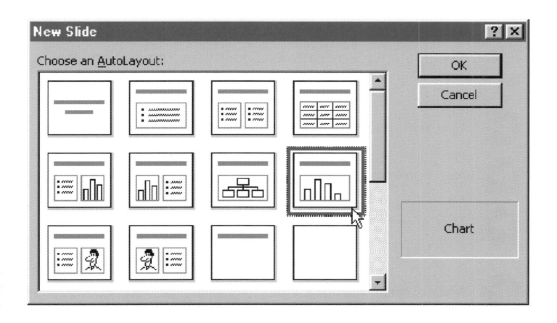

Figure 5.6: The Chart layout

 Double-click the slide to go to Slide view.

Now you are ready to begin making your chart.

 Double-click the chart placeholder that **PowerPoint** has created on the slide.

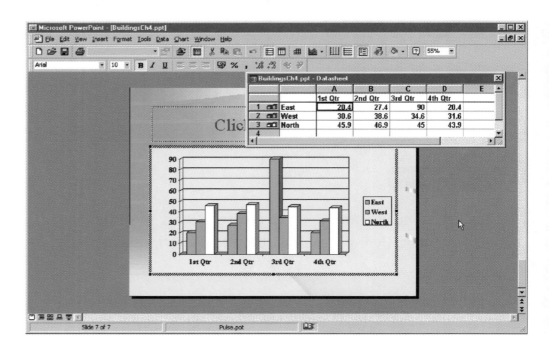

Figure 5.7: Inserting a chart into a slide

To make your chart you need to add your own information into the table.

 Click once in the cell labelled **East.**

Now begin typing **Tudor.** This will replace **East** with **Tudor.**

Click in each cell and type the row headings **Tudor, Georgian** and **Victorian** and numbers shown in Figure 5.8.

Make columns A, B and C wider by dragging the border between column headers. (See figure 5.8).

▶ Type the column headings **Village Centre, Main Village** and **Outskirts.**

▶ Delete column D by clicking the column header and pressing the **Delete** key.

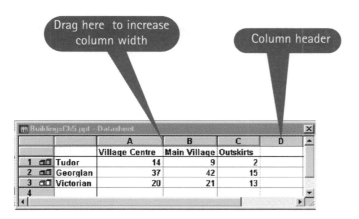

Figure 5.8: Data in the datasheet

▶ Close the table by pressing the **Close** icon. ———————

▶ Title your chart: **Number of Period Houses in Coddenham.**

▶ Click away from the heading to view the finished article.

▶ **PowerPoint** does not recognise the word **Coddenham,** so it underlines it. Right-click it and select **Ignore All.**

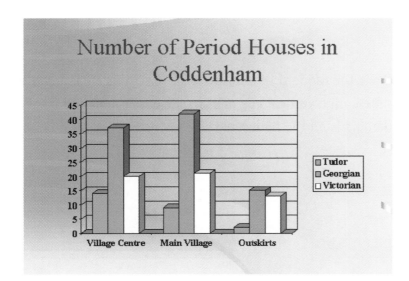

Figure 5.9: Slide featuring chart

Editing a chart

Suppose you have made a mistake in one of the figures or headings in the chart.

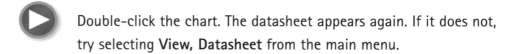 Double-click the chart. The datasheet appears again. If it does not, try selecting **View, Datasheet** from the main menu.

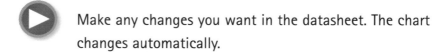 Make any changes you want in the datasheet. The chart changes automatically.

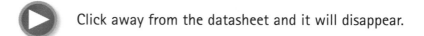 Click away from the datasheet and it will disappear.

Wrapping up

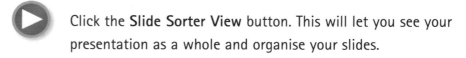 Click the **Slide Sorter View** button. This will let you see your presentation as a whole and organise your slides.

Suppose you have decided that you no longer need to explain what a modern house looks like, but would like to add a concluding slide.

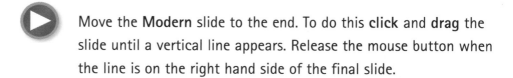 Move the **Modern** slide to the end. To do this **click** and **drag** the slide until a vertical line appears. Release the mouse button when the line is on the right hand side of the final slide.

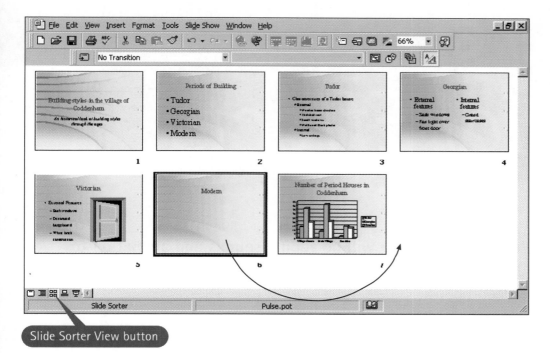

Figure 5.10: Moving slides in Slide Sorter View

In Slide view, replace **Modern** with **The End.** You can also thank your audience for coming if you wish.

To get rid of the bullet points on this slide, select the bulleted text and click **Format, bullet...** from the menu. **Un-check** the box marked **Use a bullet.**

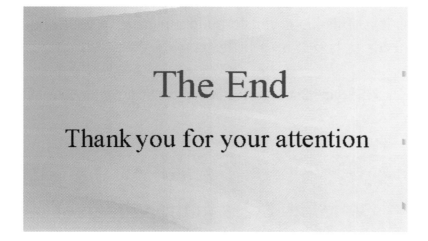

The End

Thank you for your attention

Figure 5.11: Concluding your presentation

Centre the text.

Save and **Close** your presentation.

Chapter **6**
Special Effects

In this chapter you will be adding sounds and animation to a presentation. You can also add transition effects when each screen opens.

Multimedia objects and effects, such as pictures, animation and sounds help to keep the attention of your audience.

 Open the presentation **Buildings.ppt.**

  Select the **Slide Sorter View** and click the first slide.

Viewing a slide show

Before you add any special effects to a show, it is a good idea to view it as it is. This helps you to build a picture in your mind of what it needs to jazz it up a little.

  Click the **Slide Show** button beside the Slide Sorter View button.

Building styles in the village of
Coddenham

*An historical look at building styles
through the ages*

Figure 6.1: Slide 1 in Slide Show view

Click the mouse to change to the next slide.

 Keep going until **PowerPoint** returns you to the **Slide Sorter** view.

Adding slide transitions

Transitions change the way a slide opens. You can make the next slide open like a blind or a curtain, for example.

You will notice that in **Slide Sorter** view a new Slide Sorter toolbar appears at the top of the screen. This has all the tools for adding transitions and effects to your slides.

Figure 6.2: The Slide Sorter toolbar

 With the first slide selected, click the **Slide Transition** icon at the left hand end of this toolbar.

A slide transition window opens:

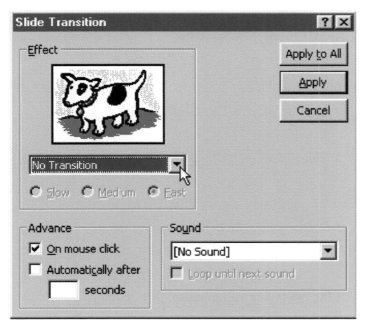

Figure 6.3: Selecting a Slide Transition

Scroll down the list and select **Split Vertical Out.** This will make the first screen open like a curtain, as if it were opening in a cinema.

You can also change the speed at which the transition occurs. In most cases, **Fast** is the best. Try experimenting!

 Click **Apply.**

 You will notice a small icon appear underneath the slide. This represents a transition action on that slide.

 **View** your changes by clicking the **Slide Show** button.

Tip:
If you click the right hand mouse button while you are viewing your show, you can select **End Show** to stop it. Or, you can simply press the **Esc** key.

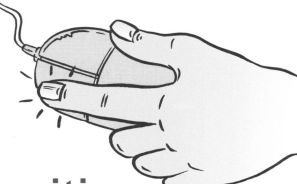

Adding transitions to multiple slides

If you wish to add a transition to all the slides, you need only click the **Apply to All** button in the Slide Transition selection box.

You can apply a transition to more than one slide but not all by selecting them first, using the **Shift** key.

To add the same transition to all the rest of the slides:

 Make sure that you are in **Slide Sorter View.**

 Click Slide 2 and then hold down the **Shift** key.

 With the **Shift** key still pressed, Click each of Slides 3 to 7.

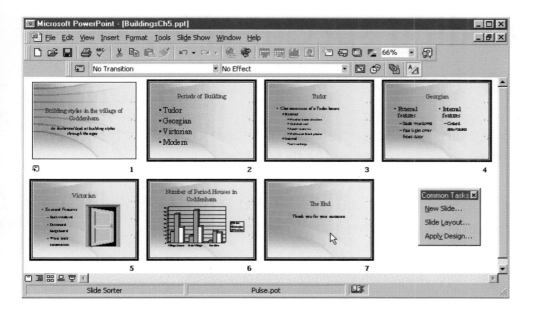

Figure 6.4: Selecting multiple slides

▶ Click the **Slide Transitions** button.

▶ Choose the **Cover Left** transition.

▶ Click **Apply.**

▶ **View** your show.

Adding Sounds

You can add a sound to accompany the transition. For example if you have a slide that pops in from one side, you could put a 'whoosh' sound in there.

▶ Click the **Slide Transition** button. ────────────────────

▶ Under the **Sound** choices, select **Whoosh.**

▶ Click **Apply to All.**

▶ **You can try out different sounds to see which ones you like.**

Adding special effects to text

PowerPoint also allows you to add animation to objects such as clip art images, charts and bulleted lists.

In **Slide Sorter View** you can add **Text Preset Animation** using the drop down menu at the top of the screen.

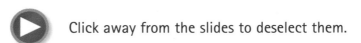 Click away from the slides to deselect them.

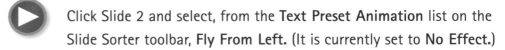 Click Slide 2 and select, from the **Text Preset Animation** list on the Slide Sorter toolbar, **Fly From Left.** (It is currently set to **No Effect.**)

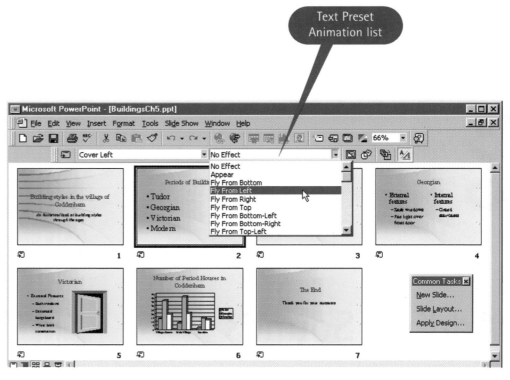

Figure 6.5 Adding text animation

You will see the animation icon appear below that slide.

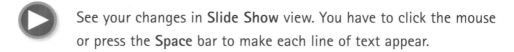 See your changes in **Slide Show** view. You have to click the mouse or press the **Space** bar to make each line of text appear.

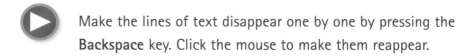 Make the lines of text disappear one by one by pressing the **Backspace** key. Click the mouse to make them reappear.

Try out some of the other **Text Preset Animations.** Some of them have sounds that go with them. Try the **Camera** option as explained below.

▶ Select Slide 7.

▶ From the main menu select **Slide Show, Preset Animation.**

▶ Select **Camera** from the submenu.

▶ Try out the effect in **Slide Show** view.

Animating objects

PowerPoint will animate an object, such as a picture or chart in the same way as it will text. However, you will need to use the **Custom Animation...** dialogue box which can be complicated. The other features of Custom Animation will not be explained in this book.

▶ Look at Slide 5 in Slide view.

▶ From the menu, select **Slide Show, Custom Animation...**

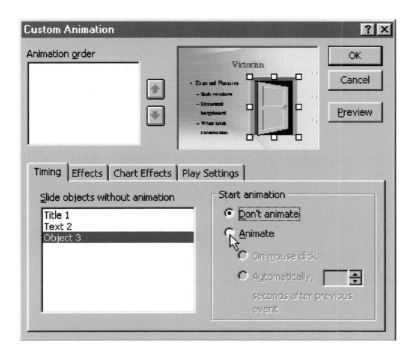

Figure 6.6: The Custom Animation dialogue box

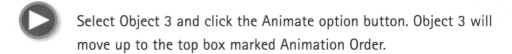 Select Object 3 and click the Animate option button. Object 3 will move up to the top box marked Animation Order.

 Click the **Effects** tab.

 Now choose your desired effect and sound (if any) and click **OK.**

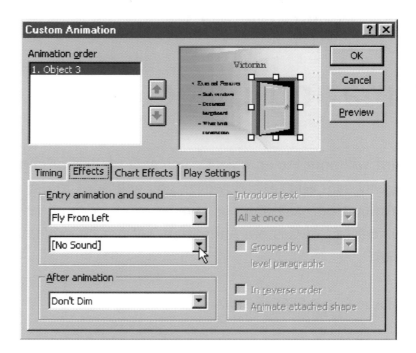 Try it out.

Figure 6.7: Choosing special effects

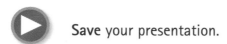 **Save** your presentation.

The **Custom Animation** feature is more complicated than most other functions in **PowerPoint** but is fun to try out.

The best way to find out more is to try building your own presentation and experiment with different transitions, effects and animations. Give it a try!

Chapter **7**
Show Time!

In this lesson you'll be finding out how **PowerPoint** can help you during your presentation. Most of these features work best when you are giving your presentation on a big screen, and controlling it from your computer. That's when **PowerPoint** presentations are most effective.

▶ Open the document called **Buildings.ppt** if it is not already open.

▶ Select the first slide.

▶ Click the **Slide Show** button. ——————————————

▶ Once in **Slide Show** mode, **right-click** the mouse and a small menu will appear.

Figure 7.1: Displaying the shortcut menu

Navigating your way around a presentation

 To find your way around a presentation you can click the **Next** and **Previous** options on the pop-up menu. This will take you to either the next or previous step in the presentation.

 If you want to move to a particular slide, click **Go** on the menu. This will bring up another menu in which you select **By Title.** Go to the **Victorian** slide.

Tip:

An easier way to go to the next slide is to click the mouse button or press the **Space bar.** To go back a slide, press the **Backspace** key.

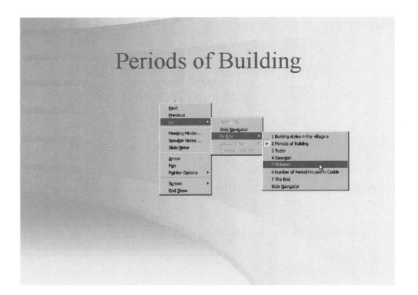

Figure 7.2: Navigation options

Using the Pen

The pen allows you to draw on the slide in freehand. This is particularly useful when explaining diagrams or graphs.

 Make sure that you are in **Slide Show** view.

 Click the right-hand mouse button and go to Slide 6, called **Number of Period Houses in Coddenham.**

Suppose you want to explain that the number of Tudor houses appears to fall at a regular rate as you move further out of the village. You can use the freehand pen to draw a trendline on the graph to help illustrate this.

▶ Click the right-hand mouse button again and click **Pointer Options.** Then click **Pen Color** on the pop-up menu.

▶ Choose **Red** or a colour that you think will show up well on the background of colours on the slide already.

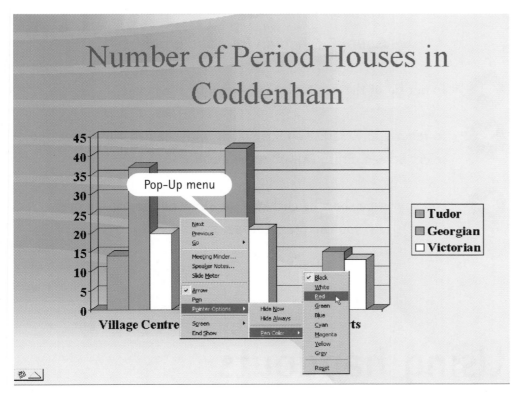

Figure 7.3: Selecting a pen colour

▶ Draw a trendline on your graph.

▶ Go to the next slide. The pen has disappeared.

▶ Make the pen appear again by right-clicking and selecting **Pen.**

▶ Experiment with different pen colours – you can draw on a single slide in many different colours!

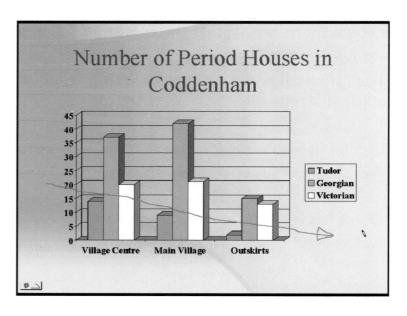

Figure 7.4: Adding freehand graphics

▶ To get rid of the pen tool, click **Arrow** on the menu.

▶ To remove any marks you have made with the pen, right-click and select **Screen, Erase Pen** from the menu.

▶ End your slide show by clicking **End Show** on the pop-up menu. Alternatively, you can press **Escape.**

Using handouts

Handouts are often useful to help the audience run through the presentation at their own pace and for writing notes on. They can also act as reminders of the main points of your presentation.

▶ Make sure that you are **not** in **Slide Show** view.

▶ From the main menu select **File, Print.**

▶ From the **Print what** menu select **Handouts (2 slides per page).**

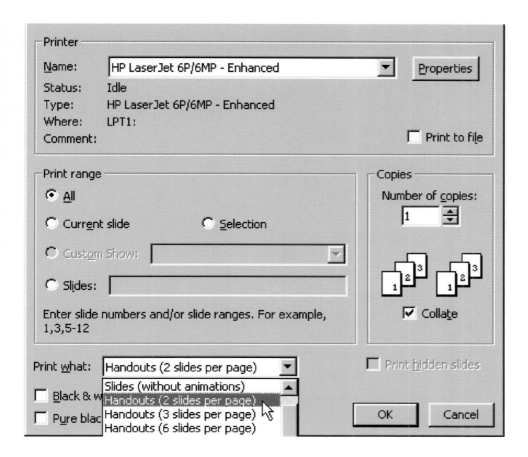

Figure 7.5: Printing handouts

▶ Click **OK.**

Using the Notes Pages

To assist you in your presentation you can make additional notes
about each slide to prompt you. These notes are visible by you
only, when you print them out or view them on screen.

▶ Select Slide 2, **Periods of Building.**

▶ Now click the **Notes Page View** button situated in the bottom left of ———
your screen.

▶ Click the area underneath the slide. Now type any notes that may be
helpful to you when delivering your presentation.

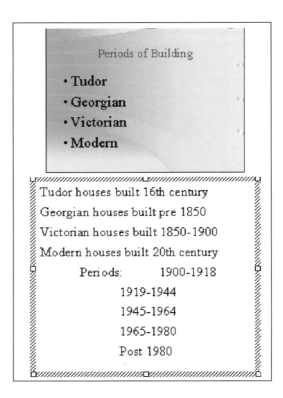

Figure 7.6: Adding notes to a slide

Viewing your notes during a presentation

You can either view the notes on screen if you get stuck for words in your show or else you can print out the Notes Pages. These are similar to the Handouts pages, except that they have all your notes attached at the bottom of each page.

 Select **Slide Show View.**

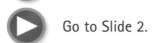 Go to Slide 2.

Click the right-hand mouse button and select **Speaker Notes...**

Your notes will appear on the screen.

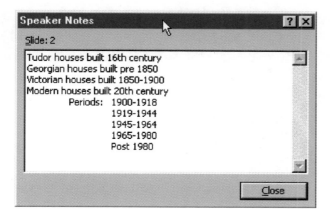

Figure 7.7: Viewing Speaker Notes during a presentation

 Press **Escape** to end your show.

Now you can print out the Notes Pages to help prompt you without having to view the notes on the screen.

 From the main menu, select **File, Print...**

 When the Print dialogue box appears, select **Notes Pages** from the **Print What** menu in the bottom left of the box. Click **OK** to print.

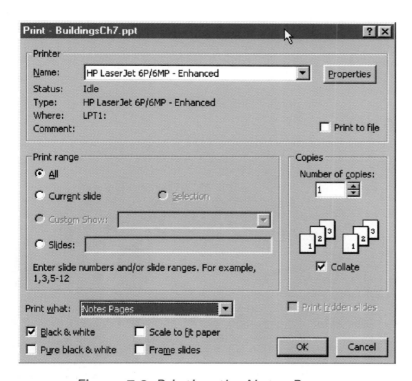

Figure 7.8: Printing the Notes Pages

You are now ready to begin delivery of your presentation.

Chapter 8
Delivery

This chapter contains tips and advice on how to deliver an effective presentation.

Presentation skills are one form of **communication skills**, and are very important all through life. They are very useful in everyday situations too, not just in front of an audience.

It is not hard to become good at presentations with a little practice and know-how.

Here are some basic tips for effective presentations to get you started.

Setting up

If you are projecting the presentation onto a wall or projector screen, you can set up the computer screen in front of you so you can see it and have the screen for the rest of the audience behind you.

Make sure the slides are readable from all seats in the room.

Rehearsals

It is a good idea to rehearse your show on your own or with your group. This will help you to time the length of the presentation and remember what you are supposed to say.

Even a quick 5-minute rehearsal can make the difference between a poor presentation and a smooth, well-timed and polished performance.

You could try rehearsing in front of a small group of friends or family to help you get used to having an audience.

Check the hardware

Arrive early to give your presentation because you need time to check the hardware. Check that you know how to operate it and that it is all working correctly.

Facing the audience

When delivering your presentation it is best not to look at the screen too often. This breaks the eye contact you will have with your audience.

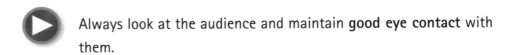 Always look at the audience and maintain **good eye contact** with them.

Speak clearly and don't rush.

Be **enthusiastic.** Look as though you are really enjoying giving this presentation, even if you aren't!

Audience Interaction

To keep the attention of the audience it is often a good idea to ask them simple questions about your presentation. Test their knowledge before you tell them the answer.

For example: **Can anyone tell me when Victorian times were?**

You can then reveal your answer: **Roughly 1850 to 1900.**

Another way to keep the audience involved is to provide handouts. But don't give out long handouts just before you start speaking, or people will read the handouts instead of listening to you. Plan carefully what you need to give them and when.

Appearance

Finally, look smart. A smart appearance can really make a statement. It draws people's attention towards you and helps them to take what you are saying more seriously.

This is one reason why business people wear suits to work every day. Of course, when you become as successful as Richard Branson you can wear what you like because everyone will want to hear you whatever you look like.

Kiosk presentations

You may be planning to give a live presentation using a computer or an overhead projector. Another option is to create a self-running presentation that people can view at a kiosk. These are often found at shopping malls and in entertainment complexes. You may decide to design a self-running presentation to run in the school entrance area or in a computer lab on a Parents' Day, for example.

▶ Make sure to have one slide selected. If no slide is selected, the following menu option will not be available.

▶ Select **Slide Show, Slide Transitions...** from the main menu. You should see the screen on the next page.

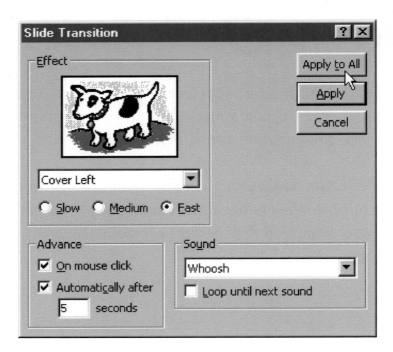

Figure 8.1: Setting up a Kiosk presentation

 From the **Advance** section of the new menu click **Automatically after? seconds.** Select **5–second** intervals.

This will now automatically flick through the slides in your show every 5 seconds. What you now need to do is loop the presentation so that when it has finished, it starts again at the beginning.

 Click the Slide Show option on the main menu and select Set Up Show... from the submenu.

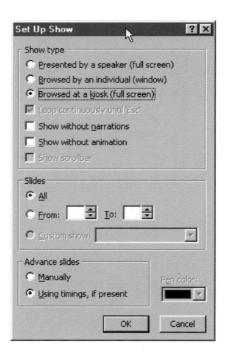

Figure 8.2: Looping your presentation

From the **Show type** category, select **Browsed at a kiosk (full screen)** from the window. Click **OK.**

This option will automatically loop the presentation until you press Escape.

Run your show!

Index